S0-BOR-439

my first book of questions and answers

early civilizations

Maggie Brown

p

This is a Parragon Publishing Book
First published in 2002

Parragon Publishing
Queen Street House
4 Queen Street
Bath BA1 1HE, UK

Produced by

David West Children's Books
7 Princeton Court
55 Felsham Road
Putney
London SW15 1AZ, UK

British Library Cataloguing-in-Publication Data

A catalogue record for this book is available from the British Library.

Hardback ISBN 0-75257-577-5
Paperback ISBN 0-75257-707-7

Printed in China

Designers
Aarti Parmar, Rob Shone, Fiona Thorne

Illustrators
Steve Caldwell, Mark Dolby, Gerry Haylock, Andy Lloyd Jones (Allied Artists)

Cartoonist
Peter Wilks (SGA)

Editor
James Pickering

CONTENTS

Who built the pyramids?

The pyramids were built by the Ancient Egyptians as magnificent tombs for their kings, the pharaohs, and other very important people. The biggest is the Great Pyramid at Giza. It was 480 feet high when it was built – taller than the Statue of Liberty is today.

Why did pharaohs need pyramids?

No one is certain, but we do know that the Egyptians believed the dead traveled to another world, the Afterlife. The sloping sides of the pyramids may have been like launch ramps, helping the pharaohs to shoot up to heaven.

Why were the Egyptians ancient?

We call them ancient because they lived so long ago – the Great Pyramid was finished in 2550 BC (before Christ was born – AD means after Christ's birth).

TRUE OR FALSE?

The pyramids had secret entrances.

TRUE. They were meant to stop robbers, but they didn't. There were over 80 pyramids – every one was robbed.

The Egyptians worshipped one god.

FALSE. They had thousands. Some paintings show gods with animal heads.

How did Egyptian men get to be mummies?

The Egyptians believed that their souls needed real bodies in the Afterlife, so they came up with ways of preserving the dead to stop them rotting away. These preserved bodies are what we call "mummies." Everybody who was anybody was mummified.

Mummification

How were mummies made?

The first stage in making a mummy was taking out the brain, lungs, heart, stomach, intestines and liver. Then the body was washed and left to dry out for 40 days in salty stuff called natron. Next up was a rub down in special oils. Finally, the body was carefully wrapped in linen bandages and put inside a nest of coffins.

TRUE OR FALSE?

Mummies were brainless.

TRUE. The brain was thrown away. The heart was put back in the body, and the other body parts were put in special stone jars.

Only people were mummified.

FALSE. Sacred animals such as cobras, crocodiles, cats and even scarab beetles were also mummified.

Who was Tutankhamun?

Tutankhamun was only 17 when he died, but he's become Egypt's best-known pharaoh. He isn't famous for what he did when he was alive, but for the glittering treasures that were buried with him – including a magnificent gold face mask and a solid gold coffin!

Tutankhamun's mask

Ancient Egyptian party

Did Egyptians throw good parties?

Pharaohs and rich people threw amazing parties, where they feasted on beef and antelope meat, and drank fine wines. There was entertainment too, from musicians, singers, dancers acrobats and even magicians.

Gazelle hunt

Who hunted hippos?

Rich Egyptian men did – they loved taking a boat out on the River Nile to hunt hippos and crocodiles. Another favorite sport was taking a racing chariot out into the desert to hunt lions, gazelles and ostriches.

TRUE OR FALSE?

All Egyptians ate beef.

FALSE. Poor people mainly ate bread, vegetables and dried fish. They drank beer.

Egyptians wore wigs.

TRUE. Pharaohs and rich people did, along with perfume, lipstick and eye makeup.

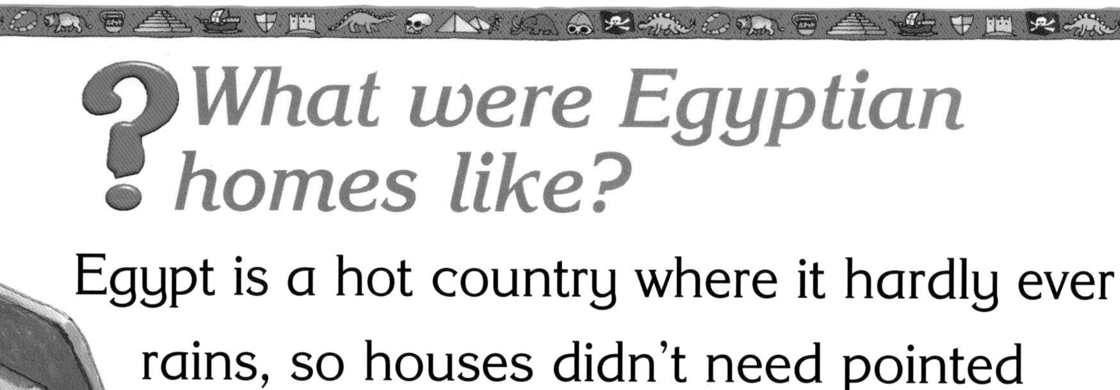

What were Egyptian homes like?

Egypt is a hot country where it hardly ever rains, so houses didn't need pointed roofs for rain to run off. Bricks were made from river mud mixed with straw and reed. Ordinary people's homes were quite small and simple, but rich people's were big with lots of rooms and a garden.

Egyptian house

Greek soldiers

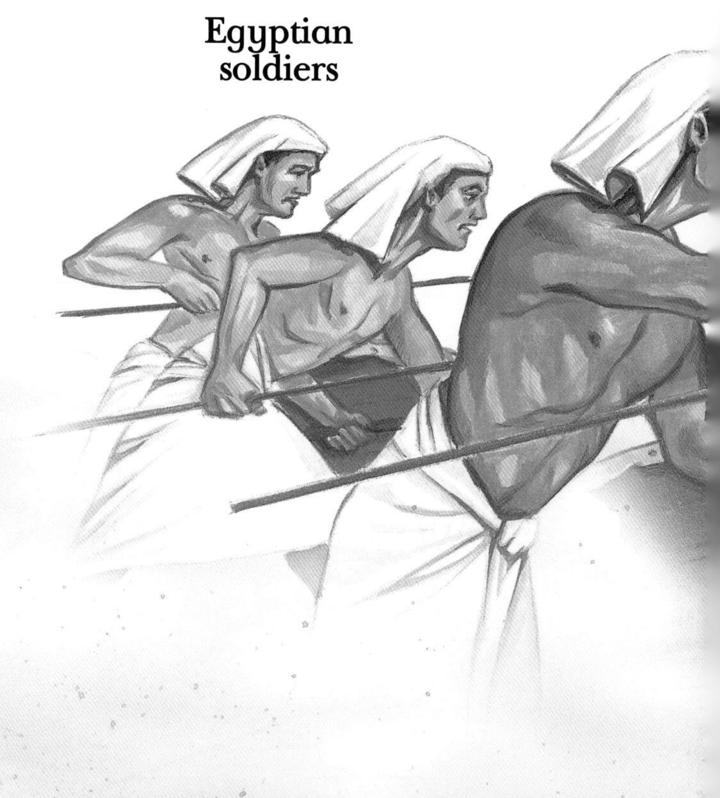

Egyptian soldiers

Did children go to school?

Boys from rich families did and, like you, they had to learn to read and write. Egyptians wrote using picture symbols called hieroglyphs, and boys had to learn 700 of them by heart.

Egyptian children

What happened to the Egyptians?

Although the Ancient Egyptians were once the most powerful nation in the world, by about 1000 BC their days of greatness were over. In 332 BC, Egypt was conquered by the Ancient Greeks and made part of their empire.

TRUE OR FALSE?

Egyptian boys left school aged 18.

FALSE. They began school aged five and left at twelve years old.

Egyptian children played with toys.

TRUE. They had balls, marbles and spinning tops, as well as toy lions and horses made of wood.

What were the Seven Wonders?

The Seven Wonders were the top spots for tourists to visit in ancient times. They were built more than 2,200 years ago.

The pyramids at Giza are the oldest of the Wonders, and the only ones still standing today.

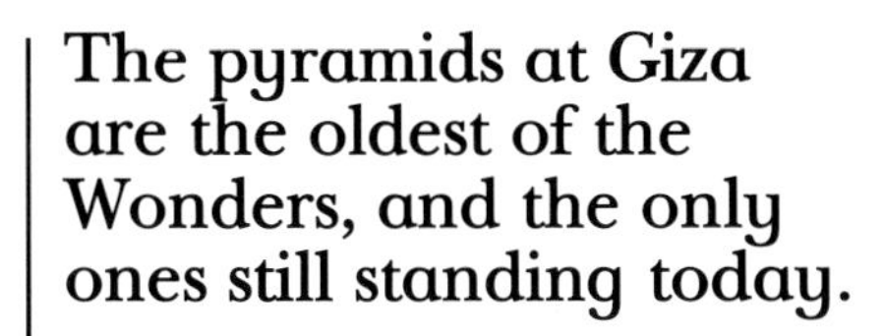

The gold and ivory Statue of Zeus at Olympia was over six times as high as a man.

The Lighthouse at Alexandria was nearly 400 feet high. The fire burning at its top could be seen by sailors far out at sea.

The Temple of Artemis at Ephesus was one of the largest temples of the ancient world.

After the pyramids, the huge Mausoleum at Halicarnassus was the most famous tomb of ancient times.

TRUE OR FALSE?

Most of the Wonders were designed by the Ancient Greeks.

TRUE. The Greeks made them all, except the Hanging Gardens and the pyramids.

The world's first zoo was in Alexandria.

TRUE. It had a leopard, a python, a giraffe and a polar bear.

Who were the Ancient Greeks?

By 700 BC, the Greek world was made up of lots of separate city-states, each formed from a city and the surrounding farmland. The biggest and most powerful city-states were Athens and Sparta.

Did the Greeks have armies?

They certainly did! The city-states were a quarrelsome lot and they often went to war. Only Sparta had a full-time army, though. The other city-states called freemen to arms when a war broke out.

Athenian soldiers

Did they have kings?

Most city-states were ruled by a king or a group of wealthy men at first. However, one of the Greeks' main claims to fame is the invention of people power. Democracy is a system of government in which people vote on how their country is run, and it was first put into practice in Athens in 508 BC.

Voting in Athens

Spartan soldiers

TRUE OR FALSE?

Athenian women helped to run cities.

FALSE. Only freemen over the age of 17 did – women and slaves weren't allowed to vote.

The biggest city-states all had navies.

TRUE. Greek warships had a vicious metal spike in front – the idea was to ram and sink enemy ships.

What did Greeks eat for breakfast?

Porridge was a favorite at breakfast time, made with barley instead of oats and livened up with figs. Lunch was usually bread and goat's cheese, while dinner might be a tasty pigeon or chicken, with fresh fruit for dessert.

Who were the toughest Greeks?

The Spartans were as tough as nails. Instead of going to ordinary school, boys were taken away from their mothers and sent to army training camps at just seven years old. To harden them up, they were kept cold and hungry and forced to go barefoot.

Spartan training camp

What did children learn at school?

Only Greek boys went to school – girls stayed at home and learned how to run a household. School subjects included reading, writing, math, music, athletics and public speaking. Schooling began when boys were 6 or 7, and lasted until they were 18-20 years old.

TRUE OR FALSE?

Greek babies had potties.

TRUE. But Greek potties were made of pottery, not plastic!

Spartan girls were wimps.

FALSE. Girls learned to run, jump and wrestle, to toughen them up for having babies later on.

When were the Olympics first held?

The first Olympic Games were held in 776 BC, to honour Zeus, the chief of the Greek gods. They were held every four years, and thousands of athletes came from all over Greece to take part.

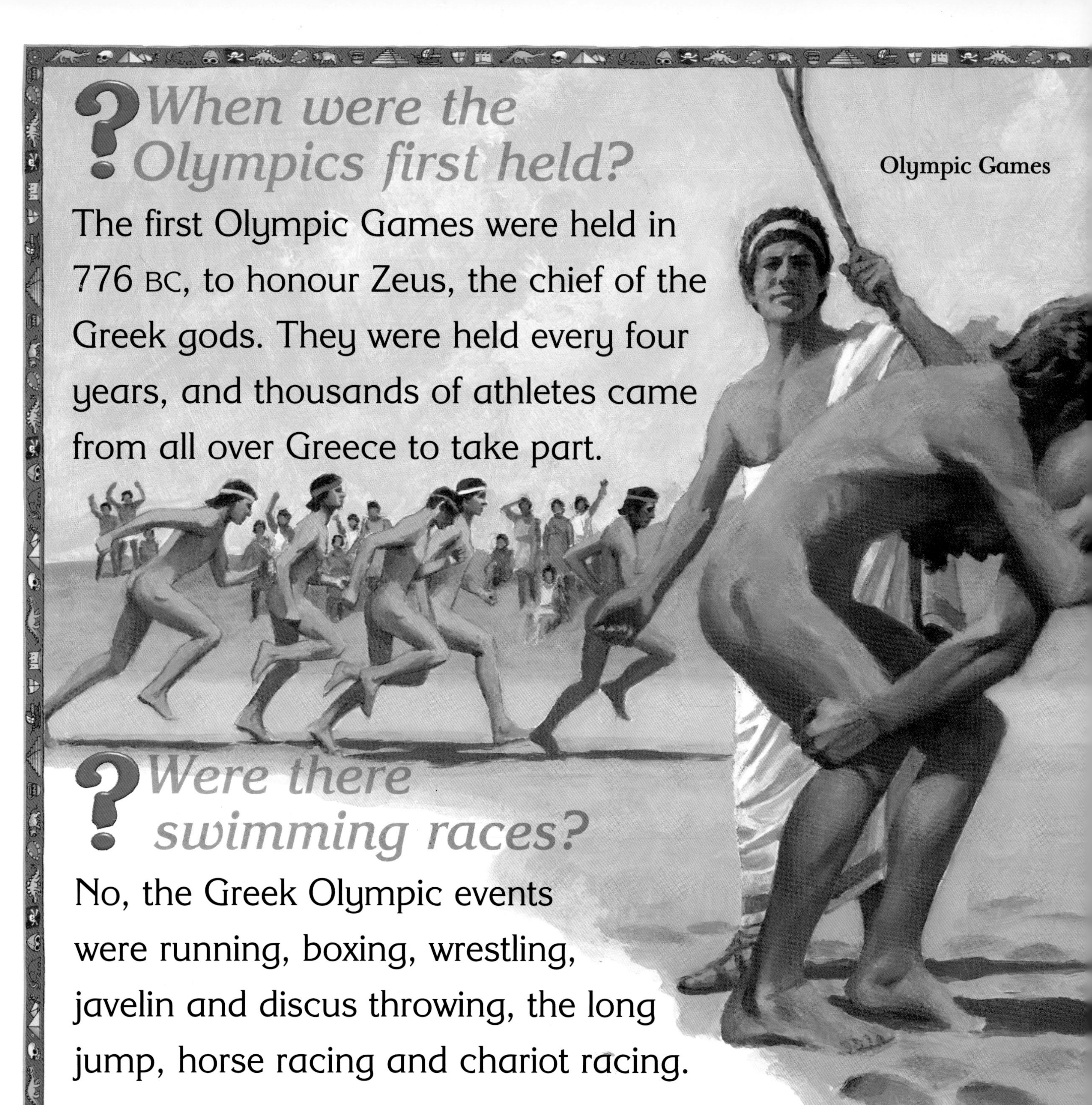

Were there swimming races?

No, the Greek Olympic events were running, boxing, wrestling, javelin and discus throwing, the long jump, horse racing and chariot racing.

Did athletes win medals?

No – winners were given small prizes at the Games, such as a crown of laurel leaves or a jar of olive oil. They were treated like superstars and showered with gifts and food when they got home, though.

Olympic champion

TRUE OR FALSE?

Greek athletes never cheated.

FALSE. Some did. If they were caught, they had to pay for a statue to be put up.

Women were banned from the Olympics.

TRUE. They held their own Games in honor of the goddess Hera, Zeus's wife.

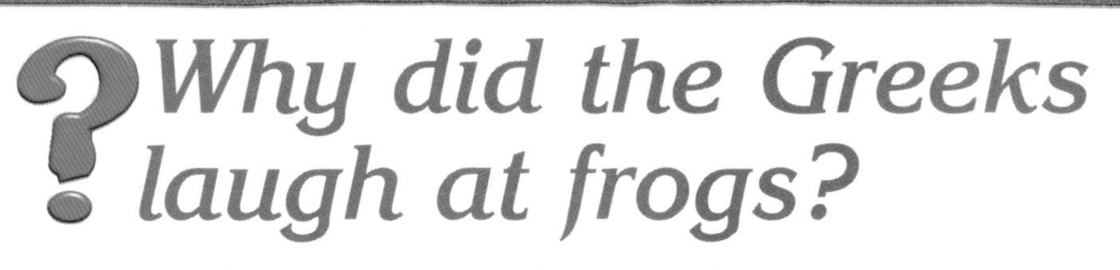

Why did the Greeks laugh at frogs?

One of the smash hit theater plays in Ancient Greek times was Frogs by the playwright Aristophanes. The Greeks were the first people to build theaters and put on plays. The theaters were open air, and the actors were all men, wearing masks painted to show which character they were playing.

Philosophers

Greek theater

Why were the Greeks wise?

The Greeks were great thinkers, who developed the art of philosophy – thinking about big questions such as the meaning of life. The most important Greek philosophers were Socrates, Plato and Aristotle.

Why was Alexander great?

Alexander the Great was a brilliant Greek general, who won a huge empire in the early 300s BC. This was the peak of Greek power. In 146 BC, the Romans took over Greece and made it part of their own empire.

Alexander the Great

TRUE OR FALSE?

The Greeks were great storytellers.

TRUE. The most famous Greek works are the Iliad and the Odyssey – tales of war, heroes, gods and mythical beings.

Zeus and Hera were the only Greek gods.

FALSE. The Greeks believed in lots of gods and goddesses, including Aphrodite, goddess of love and beauty, and Ares, the god of war.

When was Stonehenge built?

Local tribespeople began building the great stone circles of Stonehenge in southern England in about 2100 BC. The circles were built in stages, and took a lot of hard work and hundreds of years to finish – the biggest stones weigh as much as ten elephants! Experts think the tribes used Stonehenge for religious ceremonies, perhaps for worshiping the Sun and the Moon.

Stonehenge

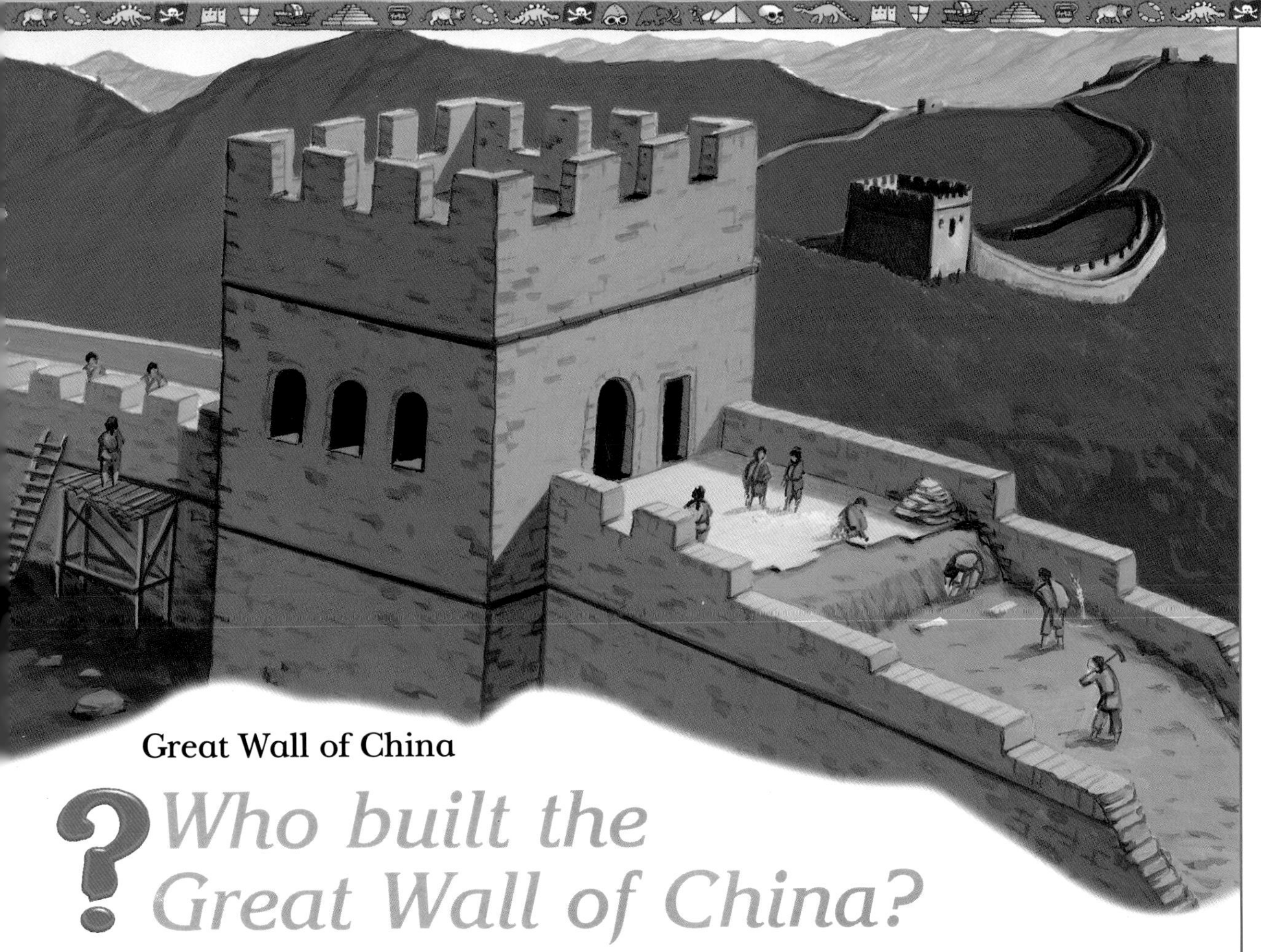

Great Wall of China

? Who built the Great Wall of China?

Shih Huang-ti was a great Chinese ruler, who was the first to conquer other Chinese leaders and govern an empire. He ordered work to start on the Great Wall in about 220 BC. After he died, he was buried in a huge tomb, with a vast army of more than 6,000 life-sized pottery statues of his warriors and their horses.

TRUE OR FALSE?

Stonehenge builders used horses and carts to shift the stones.

FALSE. The stones were brought to the site and put up using human muscle power.

The Great Wall is visible from space.

TRUE. It's the world's longest structure, at about 2,100 miles long.

Which Roman babies were looked after by a wolf?

The Romans believed that Rome, their capital city in Italy, was established in 753 BC by a man called Romulus, the son of Mars, the god of war. Roman legends also told how Romulus and his twin brother Remus were stolen from their mother when they were babies, and thrown into the River Tiber. The twins were supposed to have been saved by a wolf, who fed and cared for them as if they were her own cubs.

Romulus, Remus and the wolf

Murder of Julius Caesar

Julius Caesar

Why was Julius Caesar stabbed to death?

Julius Caesar was a Roman politician who was murdered in 44 BC by fellow politicians – they feared he wanted to overthrow the democratic government and make himself king. The Romans did end up with a kind of king though, because in 27 BC Augustus Caesar became the first Roman emperor.

TRUE OR FALSE?

Julius Caesar invaded Britain.

TRUE. He conquered France and invaded Britain twice.

Julius Caesar built Hadrian's Wall.

FALSE. The Emperor Hadrian started work on a huge stone wall across northern Britain in AD 122.

What did Roman soldiers do with tortoises?

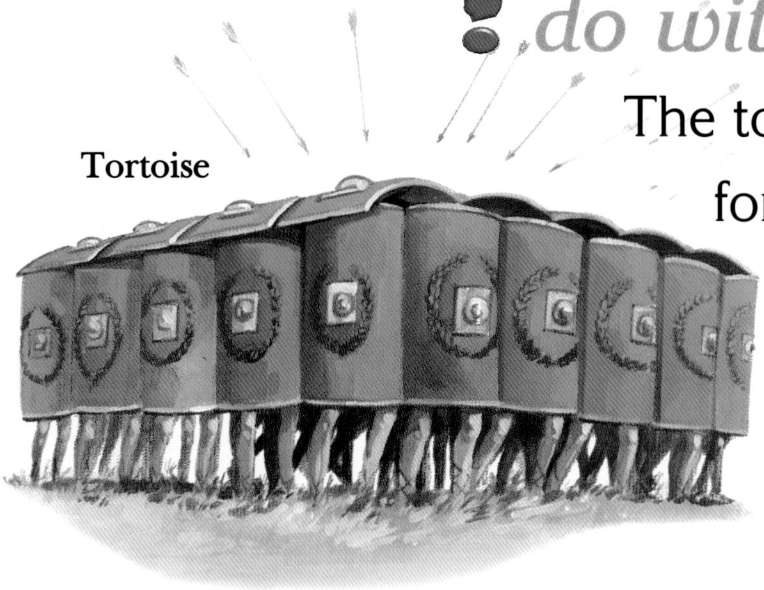

Tortoise

The tortoise was a Roman attack formation. Soldiers made a tough tortoise-shell shape around themselves with their shields, as protection against enemy weapons.

Which weapons did Roman soldiers use?

Roman soldiers fought with spears and swords. Their armor included a helmet, a breastplate and, of course, a shield.

Roman road building

What did soldiers do when they weren't fighting?

It was a tough life in the Roman army. When they weren't fighting battles, soldiers were often hard at work building roads. Engineers used special measuring tools to work out the shortest and most direct route, which is why Roman roads are famous for being straight.

TRUE OR FALSE?

The Romans invented concrete.

TRUE. The mixture was so tough that many Roman roads, bridges and buildings are still standing today.

Roman soldiers ate spaghetti.

FALSE. It hadn't been invented in Roman times. Soldiers ate bacon, cheese and biscuits.

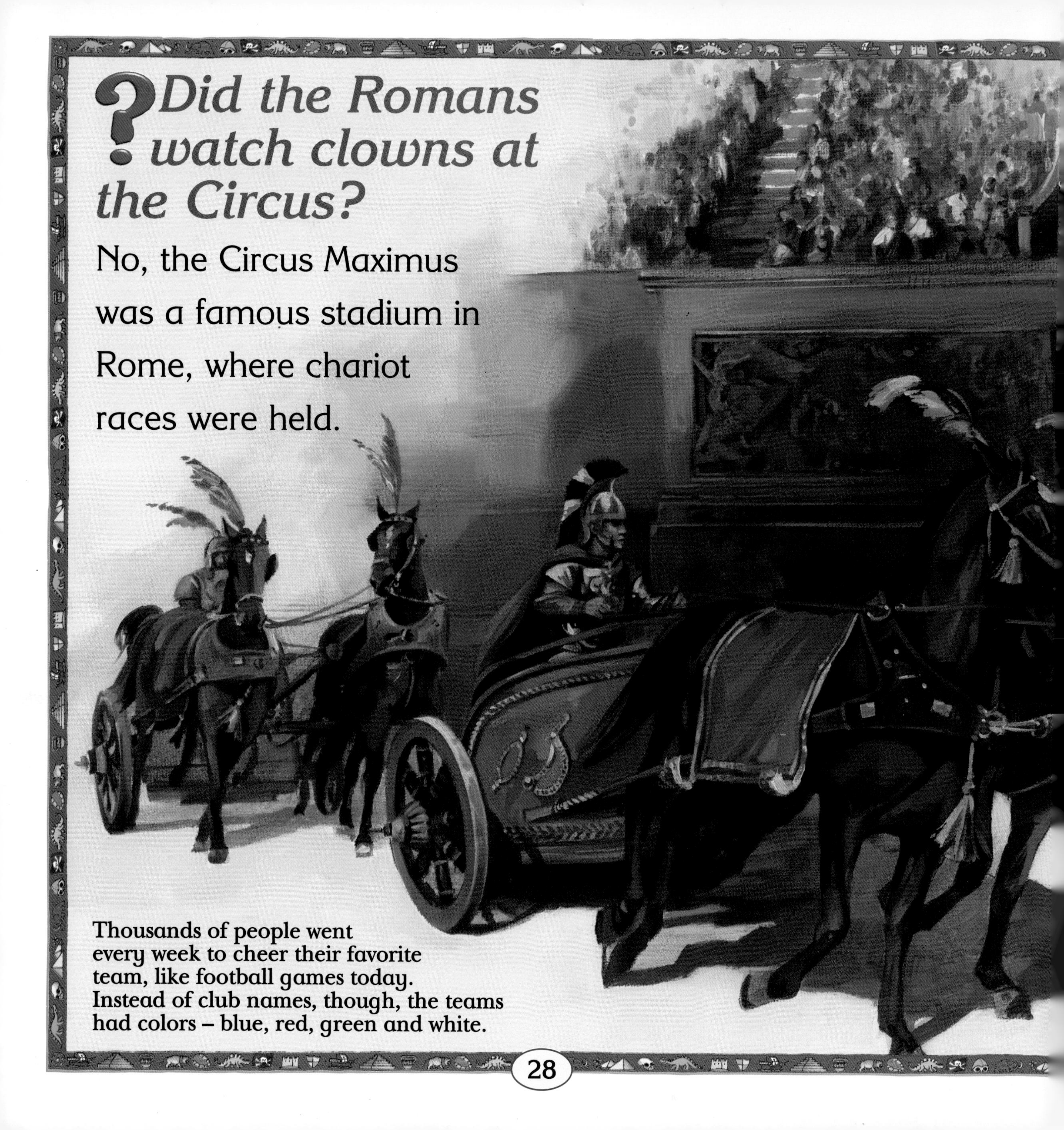

Did the Romans watch clowns at the Circus?

No, the Circus Maximus was a famous stadium in Rome, where chariot races were held.

Thousands of people went every week to cheer their favorite team, like football games today. Instead of club names, though, the teams had colors – blue, red, green and white.

Who gave the thumbs up to gladiators?

Another favorite day out was a visit to the amphitheater to watch fighters called gladiators. Usually, pairs of gladiators fought until one of them was defeated and killed. But if the crowd was in a good mood, people would give the thumbs up sign to show they wanted the loser to live.

Gladiators

TRUE OR FALSE?

Gladiators fought wild animals.

TRUE. They had to face panthers, leopards or even bears.

Only men fought as gladiators.

FALSE. Some women did. Like the men, they were criminals or war captives.

Did Romans live in apartments?

When space got tight in big cities like Rome, landlords built upward – some apartment buildings were six storeys high. Apartments were often badly built, and the ones in Rome were famous for falling down.

Roman buildings

When did girls get married?

Roman wedding

Many Roman girls were married by their 12th birthday. Girls and boys from wealthy families went to school when they were 7, but girls left at 11 years old, and boys finished some time between their 16th and 18th birthdays.

What happened to the Romans?

At the height of their power, in the AD 100s, the Romans ruled much of Europe and the Middle East, as well as the north coast of Africa. The Empire then began to crumble. It was attacked by tribes from the north and the east, and in AD 476 a Germanic warrior called Odoacer declared himself king of Italy.

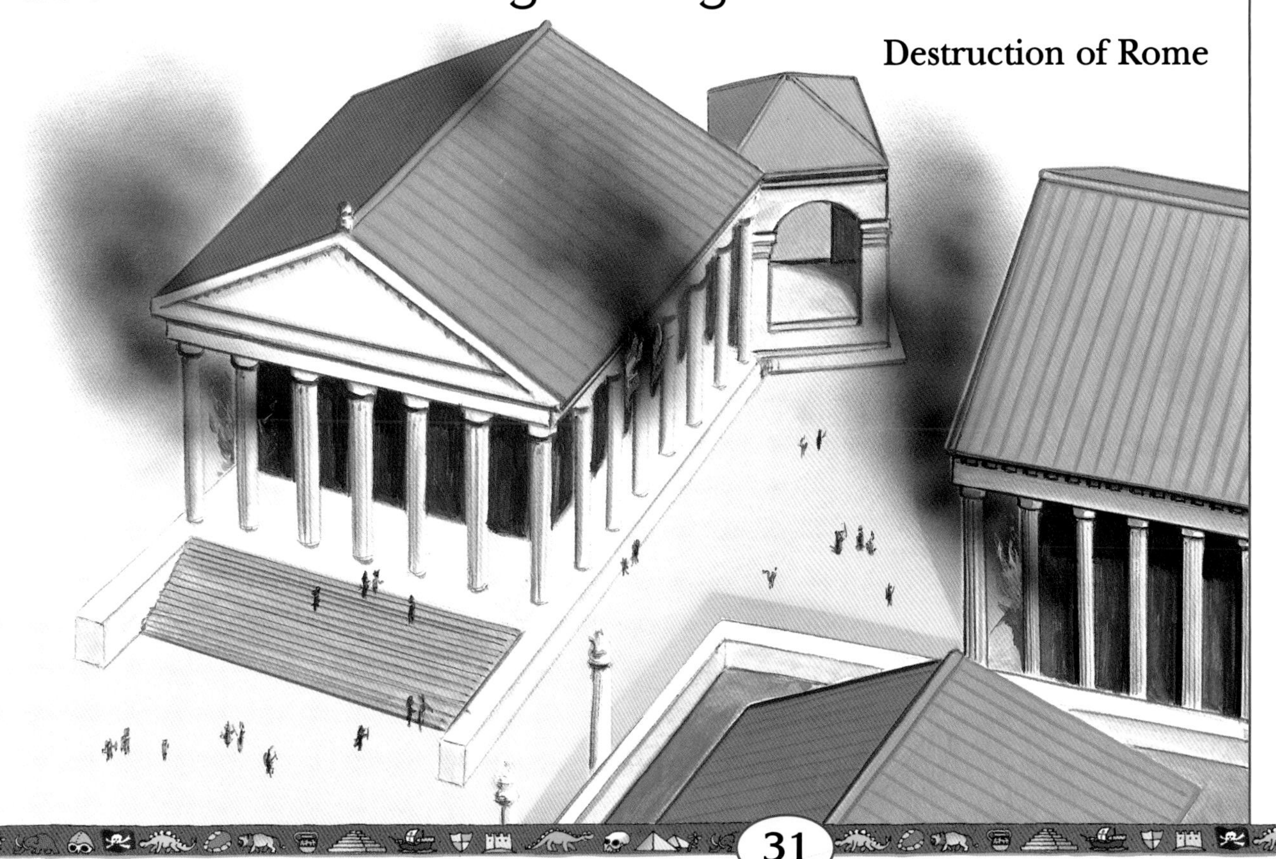
Destruction of Rome

TRUE OR FALSE?

Rich people didn't live in apartments.

TRUE. They built big luxurious villas, with underfloor heating, wall paintings and tiled floors.

The Romans ate stuffed dormice.

TRUE. Rich people had all sorts of exotic food, and they ate lying down on couches.

Index